The Constitution
of the State of Illinois:
A Quick Reference Guide

Bootblack Budget Books
Copyright 2018 ©
ISBN-13: 978-1986074155
ISBN-10: 1986074153

MAY   2018

Content:

3

Preamble

We, the People of the State of Illinois - grateful to Almighty God for the civil, political and religious liberty which He has permitted us to enjoy and seeking His blessing upon our endeavors - in order to provide for the health, safety and welfare of the people; maintain a representative and orderly government; eliminate poverty and inequality; assure legal, social and economic justice; provide opportunity for the fullest development of the individual; insure domestic tranquility; provide for the common defense; and secure the blessings of freedom and liberty to ourselves and our posterity - do ordain and establish this Constitution for the State of Illinois.

ARTICLE I: BILL OF RIGHTS

Section 1. Inherent and Inalienable Rights

All men are by nature free and independent and have certain inherent and inalienable rights among which are life, liberty and the pursuit of happiness. To secure these rights and the protection of property, governments are instituted among men, deriving their just powers from the consent of the governed.

Section 2. Due Process and Equal Protection

No person shall be deprived of life, liberty or property without due process of law nor be denied the equal protection of the laws.

Section 3. Religious Freedom

The free exercise and enjoyment of religious profession and worship, without discrimination, shall forever be guaranteed, and no person shall be denied any civil or political right, privilege or capacity, on account of his religious opinions; but the liberty of conscience hereby secured shall not be construed to dispense with oaths or affirmations, excuse acts of licentiousness, or justify practices inconsistent with the peace or safety of the State. No person shall be required to attend or support any ministry or place of worship against his consent, nor shall any preference be given by law to any religious denomination or mode of worship.

Section 4. Freedom of Speech

All persons may speak, write and publish freely, being responsible for the abuse of that liberty. In trials for libel, both civil and criminal, the truth, when published with good motives and for justifiable ends, shall be a sufficient defense.

Section 5. Right to Assemble and Petition

The people have the right to assemble in a peaceable manner, to consult for the common good, to make known their opinions to their representatives and to apply for redress of grievances.

Section 6. Searches, Seizures, Privacy and Interceptions

The people shall have the right to be secure in their persons, houses, papers and other possessions against unreasonable searches, seizures, invasions of privacy or interceptions of communications by eavesdropping devices or other means. No warrant shall issue without probable cause, supported by affidavit particularly describing the place to be searched and the persons or things to be seized.

Section 7. Indictment and Preliminary Hearing

No person shall be held to answer for a criminal offense unless on indictment of a grand jury, except in cases in which the punishment is by fine or by imprisonment other than in the penitentiary, in cases of impeachment, and in cases arising in the militia when in actual service in time of war or public danger. The General Assembly by law may abolish the grand jury or further limit its use.

No person shall be held to answer for a crime punishable by death or by imprisonment in the penitentiary unless either the initial charge has been brought by indictment of a grand jury or the person has been given a prompt preliminary hearing to establish probable cause.

Section 8. Rights after Indictment

In criminal prosecutions, the accused shall have the right to appear and defend in person and by counsel; to demand the nature and cause of the accusation and have a copy thereof; to be confronted with the witnesses against him or her and to have process to compel the attendance of witnesses in his or her behalf; and to have a speedy public trial by an impartial jury of the county in which the offense is alleged to have been committed.

Section 8.1. Crime Victims' Rights

(a) Crime victims, as defined by law, shall have the following rights:

(1) The right to be treated with fairness and respect for their dignity and privacy and to be free from harassment, intimidation, and abuse throughout the criminal justice process.

(2) The right to notice and to a hearing before a court ruling on a request for access to any of the victim's records, information, or communications which are privileged or confidential by law.

(3) The right to timely notification of all court proceedings.

(4) The right to communicate with the prosecution.

(5) The right to be heard at any post-arraignment court proceeding in which a right of the victim is at issue and any court proceeding involving a post-arraignment release decision, plea, or sentencing.

(6) The right to be notified of the conviction, the sentence, the imprisonment, and the release of the accused.

(7) The right to timely disposition of the case following the arrest of the accused.

(8) The right to be reasonably protected from the accused throughout the criminal justice process.

(9) The right to have the safety of the victim and the victim's family considered in denying or fixing the amount of bail, determining whether to release the defendant, and setting conditions of release after arrest and conviction.

(10) The right to be present at the trial and all other court proceedings on the same basis as the accused, unless the victim is to testify and the court determines that the victim's testimony would be materially affected if the victim hears other testimony at the trial.

(11) The right to have present at all court proceedings, subject to the rules of evidence, an advocate and other support person of the victim's choice.

(12) The right to restitution.

(b) The victim has standing to assert the rights enumerated in subsection (a) in any court exercising jurisdiction over the case. The court shall promptly rule on a victim's request. The victim does not have party status.

The accused does not have standing to assert the rights of a victim. The court shall not appoint an attorney for the victim under this Section. Nothing in this Section shall be construed to alter the powers, duties, and responsibilities of the prosecuting attorney.

(c) The General Assembly may provide for an assessment against convicted defendants to pay for crime victims' rights.

(d) Nothing in this Section or any law enacted under this Section creates a cause of action in equity or at law for compensation, attorney's fees, or damages against the State, a political subdivision of the State, an officer, employee, or agent of the State or of any political subdivision of the State, or an officer or employee of the court.

(e) Nothing in this Section or any law enacted under this Section shall be construed as creating

(1) a basis for vacating a conviction or

(2) a ground for any relief requested by the defendant.

Section 9. Bail and Habeas Corpus

All persons shall be bailable by sufficient sureties, except for the following offenses where the proof is evident or the presumption great: capital offenses; offenses for which a sentence of life imprisonment may be imposed as a consequence of conviction; and felony offenses for which a sentence of imprisonment, without conditional and revocable release, shall be imposed by law as a consequence of conviction, when the court, after a hearing, determines that release of the offender would pose a real and present threat to the physical safety of any person. The privilege of the writ of habeas corpus shall not be suspended except in cases of rebellion or invasion when the public safety may require it.

Any costs accruing to a unit of local government as a result of the denial of bail pursuant to the 1986 Amendment to this Section shall be reimbursed by the State to the unit of local government.

Section 10. Self-Incrimination and Double Jeopardy

No person shall be compelled in a criminal case to give evidence against himself nor be twice put in jeopardy for the same offense.

Section 11. Limitation of Penalties after Conviction

All penalties shall be determined both according to the seriousness of the offense and with the objective of restoring the offender to useful citizenship. No conviction shall work corruption of blood or forfeiture of estate. No person shall be transported out of the State for an offense committed within the State.

Section 12. Right to Remedy and Justice

Every person shall find a certain remedy in the laws for all injuries and wrongs which he receives to his person, privacy, property or reputation. He shall obtain justice by law, freely, completely, and promptly.

Section 13. Trial by Jury

The right of trial by jury as heretofore enjoyed shall remain inviolate.

Section 14. Imprisonment for Debt

No person shall be imprisoned for debt unless he refuses to deliver up his estate for the benefit of his creditors as provided by law or unless there is a strong presumption of fraud. No person shall be imprisoned for failure to pay a fine in a criminal case unless he has been afforded adequate time to make payment, in installments if necessary, and has willfully failed to make payment.

Section 15. Right of Eminent Domain

Private property shall not be taken or damaged for public use without just compensation as provided by law. Such compensation shall be determined by a jury as provided by law.

Section 16. Ex Post Facto Laws and Impairing Contracts

No ex post facto law, or law impairing the obligation of contracts or making an irrevocable grant of special privileges or immunities, shall be passed.

Section 17. No Discrimination in Employment and the Sale or Rental of Property

All persons shall have the right to be free from discrimination on the basis of race, color, creed, national ancestry and sex in the hiring and promotion practices of any employer or in the sale or rental of property.

These rights are enforceable without action by the General Assembly, but the General Assembly by law may establish reasonable exemptions relating to these rights and provide additional remedies for their violation.

Section 18. No Discrimination on the Basis of Sex

The equal protection of the laws shall not be denied or abridged on account of sex by the State or its units of local government and school districts.

Section 19. No Discrimination Against the Handicapped

All persons with a physical or mental handicap shall be free from discrimination in the sale or rental of property and shall be free from discrimination unrelated to ability in the hiring and promotion practices of any employer.

Section 20. Individual Dignity

To promote individual dignity, communications that portray criminality, depravity or lack of virtue in, or that incite violence, hatred, abuse or hostility toward, a person or group of persons by reason of or by reference to religious, racial, ethnic, national or regional affiliation are condemned.

Section 21. Quartering of Soldiers

No soldier in time of peace shall be quartered in a house without the consent of the owner; nor in time of war except as provided by law.

Section 22. Right to Arms

Subject only to the police power, the right of the individual citizen to keep and bear arms shall not be infringed.

Section 23. Fundamental Principles

A frequent recurrence to the fundamental principles of civil government is necessary to preserve the blessings of liberty. These blessings cannot endure unless the people recognize their corresponding individual obligations and responsibilities.

Section 24. Rights Retained

The enumeration in this Constitution of certain rights shall not be construed to deny or disparage others retained by the individual citizens of the State.

ARTICLE II: THE POWERS OF THE STATE

Section 1. Separation of Powers

The legislative, executive and judicial branches are separate. No branch shall exercise powers properly belonging to another.

Section 2. Powers of Government

The enumeration in this Constitution of specified powers and functions shall not be construed as a limitation of powers of state government.

ARTICLE III: SUFFRAGE AND ELECTIONS

Section 1. Voting Qualifications

Every United States citizen who has attained the age of
18 or any other voting age required by the United States for
voting in State elections and who has been a permanent
resident of this State for at least 30 days next preceding
any election shall have the right to vote at such election.
The General Assembly by law may establish registration
requirements and require permanent residence in an election
district not to exceed thirty days prior to an election. The
General Assembly by law may establish shorter residence
requirements for voting for President and Vice-President of
the United States.

Section 2. Voting Disqualifications

A person convicted of a felony, or otherwise under sentence in a
correctional institution or jail, shall lose the right to vote, which
right shall be restored not later than upon completion of his
sentence.

Section 3. Elections

All elections shall be free and equal.

Section 4. Election Laws

The General Assembly by law shall define permanent residence
for voting purposes, insure secrecy of voting and the integrity of
the election process, and facilitate registration and voting by all
qualified persons. Laws governing voter registration and conduct
of elections shall be general and uniform.

Section 5. Board of Elections

A State Board of Elections shall have general supervision over the administration of the registration and election laws throughout the State. The General Assembly by law shall determine the size, manner of selection and compensation of the Board. No political party shall have a majority of members of the Board.

Section 6. General Election

As used in all articles of this Constitution except Article VII, "general election" means the biennial election at which members of the General Assembly are elected. Such election shall be held on the Tuesday following the first Monday of November in even-numbered years or on such other day as provided by law.

Section 7. Initiative to Recall Governor

(a) The recall of the Governor may be proposed by a petition signed by a number of electors equal in number to at least 15% of the total votes cast for Governor in the preceding gubernatorial election, with at least 100 signatures from each of at least 25 separate counties. A petition shall have been signed by the petitioning electors not more than 150 days after an affidavit has been filed with the State Board of Elections providing notice of intent to circulate a petition to recall the Governor. The affidavit may be filed no sooner than 6 months after the beginning of the Governor's term of office. The affidavit shall have been signed by the proponent of the recall petition, at least 20 members of the House of Representatives, and at least 10 members of the Senate, with no more than half of the signatures of members of each chamber from the same established political party.

(b) The form of the petition, circulation, and procedure for determining the validity and sufficiency of a petition shall be as provided by law. If the petition is valid and sufficient, the State Board of Elections shall certify the petition not more than 100 days after the date the petition was filed, and the question "Shall (name) be recalled from the office of Governor?" must be submitted to the electors at a special election called by the State Board of Elections, to occur not more than 100 days after certification of the petition. A recall petition certified by the State Board of Elections may not be withdrawn and another recall petition may not be initiated against the Governor during the remainder of the current term of office. Any recall petition or recall election pending on the date of the next general election at which a candidate for Governor is elected is moot.

(c) If a petition to recall the Governor has been filed with the State Board of Elections, a person eligible to serve as Governor may propose his or her candidacy by a petition signed by a number of electors equal in number to the requirement for petitions for an established party candidate for the office of Governor, signed by petitioning electors not more than 50 days after a recall petition has been filed with the State Board of Elections. The form of a successor election petition, circulation, and procedure for determining the validity and sufficiency of a petition shall be as provided by law. If the successor election petition is valid and sufficient, the State Board of Elections shall certify the petition not more than 100 days after the date the petition to recall the Governor was filed. Names of candidates for nomination to serve as the candidate of an established political party must be submitted to the electors at a special primary election, if necessary, called by the State Board of Elections to be held at the same time as the special election on the question of recall established under subsection (b). Names of candidates for the successor election must be submitted to the electors at a special successor election called by the State Board of Elections, to occur not more than 60 days after the date of the special primary election or on a date established by law.

(d) The Governor is immediately removed upon certification of the recall election results if a majority of the electors voting on the question vote to recall the Governor. If the Governor is removed, then:

(i) an Acting Governor determined under subsection (a) of Section 6 of Article V shall serve until the Governor elected at the special successor election is qualified and

(ii) the candidate who receives the highest number of votes in the special successor election is elected Governor for the balance of the term.

Section 8. Voter Discrimination

No person shall be denied the right to register to vote or to cast a ballot in an election based on race, color, ethnicity, status as a member of a language minority, national origin, religion, sex, sexual orientation, or income.

ARTICLE IV: THE LEGISLATURE

Section 1. Legislature - Power and Structure

The legislative power is vested in a General Assembly consisting of a Senate and a House of Representatives, elected by the electors from 59 Legislative Districts and 118 Representative Districts.

Section 2. Legislative Composition

(a) One Senator shall be elected from each Legislative District. Immediately following each decennial redistricting, the General Assembly by law shall divide the Legislative Districts as equally as possible into three groups. Senators from one group shall be elected for terms of four years, four years and two years; Senators from the second group, for terms of four years, two years and four years; and Senators from the third group, for terms of two years, four years and four years. The Legislative Districts in each group shall be distributed substantially equally over the State.

(b) Each Legislative District shall be divided into two Representative Districts. In 1982 and every two years thereafter one Representative shall be elected from each Representative District for a term of two years.

(c) To be eligible to serve as a member of the General Assembly, a person must be a United States citizen, at least 21 years old, and for the two years preceding his election or appointment a resident of the district which he is to represent. In the general election following a redistricting, a candidate for the General Assembly may be elected from any district which contains a part of the district in which he resided at the time of the redistricting and reelected if a resident of the new district he represents for 18 months prior to reelection.

(d) Within thirty days after a vacancy occurs, it shall be filled by appointment as provided by law. If the vacancy is in a Senatorial office with more than twenty-eight months remaining in the term, the appointed Senator shall serve until the next general election, at which time a Senator shall be elected to serve for the remainder of the term. If the vacancy is in a Representative office or in any other Senatorial office, the appointment shall be for the remainder of the term. An appointee to fill a vacancy shall be a member of the same political party as the person he succeeds.

(e) No member of the General Assembly shall receive compensation as a public officer or employee from any other governmental entity for time during which he is in attendance as a member of the General Assembly.

No member of the General Assembly during the term for which he was elected or appointed shall be appointed to a public office which shall have been created or the compensation for which shall have been increased by the General Assembly during that term.

Section 3. Legislative Redistricting

(a) Legislative Districts shall be compact, contiguous and substantially equal in population. Representative Districts shall be compact, contiguous, and substantially equal in population.

(b) In the year following each Federal decennial census year, the General Assembly by law shall redistrict the Legislative Districts and the Representative Districts.

If no redistricting plan becomes effective by June 30 of that year, a Legislative Redistricting Commission shall be constituted not later than July 10. The Commission shall consist of eight members, no more than four of whom shall be members of the same political party. The Speaker and Minority Leader of the House of Representatives shall each appoint to the Commission one Representative and one person who is not a member of the General Assembly. The President and Minority Leader of the Senate shall each appoint to the Commission one Senator and one person who is not a member of the General Assembly.

The members shall be certified to the Secretary of State by the appointing authorities. A vacancy on the Commission shall be filled within five days by the authority that made the original appointment. A Chairman and Vice Chairman shall be chosen by a majority of all members of the Commission.

Not later than August 10, the Commission shall file with the Secretary of State a redistricting plan approved by at least five members.

If the Commission fails to file an approved redistricting plan, the Supreme Court shall submit the names of two persons, not of the same political party, to the Secretary of State not later than September 1.

Not later than September 5, the Secretary of State publicly shall draw by random selection the name of one of the two persons to serve as the ninth member of the Commission.

Not later than October 5, the Commission shall file with the Secretary of State a redistricting plan approved by at least five members.

An approved redistricting plan filed with the Secretary of State shall be presumed valid, shall have the force and effect of law and shall be published promptly by the Secretary of State.

The Supreme Court shall have original and exclusive jurisdiction over actions concerning redistricting the House and Senate, which shall be initiated in the name of the People of the State by the Attorney General.

Section 4. Election

Members of the General Assembly shall be elected at the general election in even-numbered years.

Section 5. Sessions

(a) The General Assembly shall convene each year on the second Wednesday of January. The General Assembly shall be a continuous body during the term for which members of the House of Representatives are elected.

(b) The Governor may convene the General Assembly or the Senate alone in special session by a proclamation stating the purpose of the session; and only business encompassed by such purpose, together with any impeachments or confirmation of appointments shall be transacted. Special sessions of the General Assembly may also be convened by joint proclamation of the presiding officers of both houses, issued as provided by law.

(c) Sessions of each house of the General Assembly and meetings of committees, joint committees and legislative commissions shall be open to the public. Sessions and committee meetings of a house may be closed to the public if two-thirds of the members elected to that house determine that the public interest so requires; and meetings of joint committees and legislative commissions may be so closed if two-thirds of the members elected to each house so determine.

Section 6. Organization

(a) A majority of the members elected to each house constitutes a quorum.

(b) On the first day of the January session of the General Assembly in odd-numbered years, the Secretary of State shall convene the House of Representatives to elect from its membership a Speaker of the House of Representatives as presiding officer, and the Governor shall convene the Senate to elect from its membership a President of the Senate as presiding officer.

(c) For purposes of powers of appointment conferred by this Constitution, the Minority Leader of either house is a member of the numerically strongest political party other than the party to which the Speaker or the President belongs, as the case may be.

(d) Each house shall determine the rules of its proceedings, judge the elections, returns and qualifications of its members and choose its officers. No member shall be expelled by either house, except by a vote of two-thirds of the members elected to that house. A member may be expelled only once for the same offense. Each house may punish by imprisonment any person, not a member, guilty of disrespect to the house by disorderly or contemptuous behavior in its presence. Imprisonment shall not extend beyond twenty-four hours at one time unless the person persists in disorderly or contemptuous behavior.

Section 7. Transaction of Business

(a) Committees of each house, joint committees of the two houses and legislative commissions shall give reasonable public notice of meetings, including a statement of subjects to be considered.

(b) Each house shall keep a journal of its proceedings and a transcript of its debates. The journal shall be published and the transcript shall be available to the public.

(c) Either house or any committee thereof as provided by law may compel by subpoena the attendance and testimony of witnesses and the production of books, records and papers.

Section 8. Passage of Bills

(a) The enacting clause of the laws of this State shall be: "Be it enacted by the People of the State of Illinois, represented in the General Assembly."

(b) The General Assembly shall enact laws only by bill. Bills may originate in either house, but may be amended or rejected by the other.

(c) No bill shall become a law without the concurrence of a majority of the members elected to each house. Final passage of a bill shall be by record vote. In the Senate at the request of two members, and in the House at the request of five members, a record vote may be taken on any other occasion. A record vote is a vote by yeas and nays entered on the journal.

(d) A bill shall be read by title on three different days in each house. A bill and each amendment thereto shall be reproduced and placed on the desk of each member before final passage.

Bills, except bills for appropriations and for the codification, revision or rearrangement of laws, shall be confined to one subject. Appropriation bills shall be limited to the subject of appropriations.

A bill expressly amending a law shall set forth completely the sections amended.

The Speaker of the House of Representatives and the President of the Senate shall sign each bill that passes both houses to certify that the procedural requirements for passage have been met.

Section 9. Veto Procedure

(a) Every bill passed by the General Assembly shall be presented to the Governor within 30 calendar days after its passage. The foregoing requirement shall be judicially enforceable. If the Governor approves the bill, he shall sign it and it shall become law.

(b) If the Governor does not approve the bill, he shall veto it by returning it with his objections to the house in which it originated. Any bill not so returned by the Governor within 60 calendar days after it is presented to him shall become law. If recess or adjournment of the General Assembly prevents the return of a bill, the bill and the Governor's objections shall be filed with the Secretary of State within such 60 calendar days. The Secretary of State shall return the bill and objections to the originating house promptly upon the next meeting of the same General Assembly at which the bill can be considered.

(c) The house to which a bill is returned shall immediately enter the Governor's objections upon its journal. If within 15 calendar days after such entry that house by a record vote of three-fifths of the members elected passes the bill, it shall be delivered immediately to the second house. If within 15 calendar days after such delivery the second house by a record vote of three-fifths of the members elected passes the bill, it shall become law.

(d) The Governor may reduce or veto any item of appropriations in a bill presented to him. Portions of a bill not reduced or vetoed shall become law. An item vetoed shall be returned to the house in which it originated and may become law in the same manner as a vetoed bill. An item reduced in amount shall be returned to the house in which it originated and may be restored to its original amount in the same manner as a vetoed bill except that the required record vote shall be a majority of the members elected to each house. If a reduced item is not so restored, it shall become law in the reduced amount.

(e) The Governor may return a bill together with specific recommendations for change to the house in which it originated. The bill shall be considered in the same manner as a vetoed bill but the specific recommendations may be accepted by a record vote of a majority of the members elected to each house. Such bill shall be presented again to the Governor and if he certifies that such acceptance conforms to his specific recommendations, the bill shall become law. If he does not so certify, he shall return it as a vetoed bill to the house in which it originated.

Section 10. Effective Date of Laws

The General Assembly shall provide by law for a uniform effective date for laws passed prior to June 1 of a calendar year. The General Assembly may provide for a different effective date in any law passed prior to June 1. A bill passed after May 31 shall not become effective prior to June 1 of the next calendar year unless the General Assembly by the vote of three-fifths of the members elected to each house provides for an earlier effective date.

Section 11. Compensation and Allowances

A member shall receive a salary and allowances as provided by law, but changes in the salary of a member shall not take effect during the term for which he has been elected.

Section 12. Legislative Immunity

Except in cases of treason, felony or breach of peace, a member shall be privileged from arrest going to, during, and returning from sessions of the General Assembly. A member shall not be held to answer before any other tribunal for any speech or debate, written or oral, in either house. These immunities shall apply to committee and legislative commission proceedings.

Section 13. Special Legislation

The General Assembly shall pass no special or local law when a general law is or can be made applicable. Whether a general law is or can be made applicable shall be a matter for judicial determination.

Section 14. Impeachment

The House of Representatives has the sole power to conduct legislative investigations to determine the existence of cause for impeachment and, by the vote of a majority of the members elected, to impeach Executive and Judicial officers. Impeachments shall be tried by the Senate. When sitting for that purpose, Senators shall be upon oath, or affirmation, to do justice according to law. If the Governor is tried, the Chief Justice of the Supreme Court shall preside. No person shall be convicted without the concurrence of two-thirds of the Senators elected. Judgment shall not extend beyond removal from office and disqualification to hold any public office of this State. An impeached officer, whether convicted or acquitted, shall be liable to prosecution, trial, judgment and punishment according to law.

Section 15. Adjournment

(a) When the General Assembly is in session, neither house without the consent of the other shall adjourn for more than three days or to a place other than where the two houses are sitting.

(b) If either house certifies that a disagreement exists between the houses as to the time for adjourning a session, the Governor may adjourn the General Assembly to a time not later than the first day of the next annual session.

ARTICLE V: THE EXECUTIVE

Section 1. Officers

The Executive Branch shall include a Governor, Lieutenant Governor, Attorney General, Secretary of State, Comptroller and Treasurer elected by the electors of the State. They shall keep the public records and maintain a residence at the seat of government during their terms of office.

Section 2. Terms

These elected officers of the Executive Branch shall hold office for four years beginning on the second Monday of January after their election and, except in the case of the Lieutenant Governor, until their successors are qualified. They shall be elected at the general election in 1978 and every four years thereafter.

Section 3. Eligibility

To be eligible to hold the office of Governor, Lieutenant Governor, Attorney General, Secretary of State, Comptroller or Treasurer, a person must be a United States citizen, at least 25 years old, and a resident of this State for the three years preceding his election.

Section 4. Joint Election

In the general election for Governor and Lieutenant Governor, one vote shall be cast jointly for the candidates nominated by the same political party or petition. The General Assembly may provide by law for the joint nomination of candidates for Governor and Lieutenant Governor.

Section 5. Canvass - Contests

The election returns for executive offices shall be
sealed and transmitted to the Secretary of State, or other
person or body provided by law, who shall examine and
consolidate the returns. The person having the highest number
of votes for an office shall be declared elected. If two or
more persons have an equal and the highest number of votes
for an office, they shall draw lots to determine which of
them shall be declared elected. Election contests shall be
decided by the courts in a manner provided by law.

Section 6. Gubernatorial Succession

(a) In the event of a vacancy, the order of succession
to the office of Governor or to the position of Acting
Governor shall be the Lieutenant Governor, the elected
Attorney General, the elected Secretary of State, and then as
provided by law.

(b) If the Governor is unable to serve because of death,
conviction on impeachment, failure to qualify, resignation or
other disability, the office of Governor shall be filled by
the officer next in line of succession for the remainder of
the term or until the disability is removed.

(c) Whenever the Governor determines that he may be
seriously impeded in the exercise of his powers, he shall so
notify the Secretary of State and the officer next in line of
succession. The latter shall thereafter become Acting
Governor with the duties and powers of Governor. When the
Governor is prepared to resume office, he shall do so by
notifying the Secretary of State and the Acting Governor.

(d) The General Assembly by law shall specify by whom
and by what procedures the ability of the Governor to serve
or to resume office may be questioned and determined. The
Supreme Court shall have original and exclusive jurisdiction

to review such a law and any such determination and, in the absence of such a law, shall make the determination under such rules as it may adopt.

Section 7. Vacancies in Other Elective Offices

If the Attorney General, Secretary of State, Comptroller or Treasurer fails to qualify or if his office becomes vacant, the Governor shall fill the office by appointment. The appointee shall hold office until the elected officer qualifies or until a successor is elected and qualified as may be provided by law and shall not be subject to removal by the Governor. If the Lieutenant Governor fails to qualify or if his office becomes vacant, it shall remain vacant until the end of the term.

Section 8. Governor - Supreme Executive Power

The Governor shall have the supreme executive power, and shall be responsible for the faithful execution of the laws.

Section 9. Governor - Appointing Power

(a) The Governor shall nominate and, by and with the advice and consent of the Senate, a majority of the members elected concurring by record vote, shall appoint all officers whose election or appointment is not otherwise provided for. Any nomination not acted upon by the Senate within 60 session days after the receipt thereof shall be deemed to have received the advice and consent of the Senate. The General Assembly shall have no power to elect or appoint officers of the Executive Branch.

(b) If, during a recess of the Senate, there is a vacancy in an office filled by appointment by the Governor by and with the advice and consent of the Senate, the Governor shall make a temporary appointment until the next meeting of the Senate, when he shall make a nomination to fill such office.

(c) No person rejected by the Senate for an office shall, except at the Senate's request, be nominated again for that office at the same session or be appointed to that office during a recess of that Senate.

Section 10. Governor - Removals

The Governor may remove for incompetence, neglect of duty, or malfeasance in office any officer who may be appointed by the Governor.

Section 11. Governor - Agency Reorganization

The Governor, by Executive Order, may reassign functions among or reorganize executive agencies which are directly responsible to him. If such a reassignment or reorganization would contravene a statute, the Executive Order shall be delivered to the General Assembly. If the General Assembly is in annual session and if the Executive Order is delivered on or before April 1, the General Assembly shall consider the Executive Order at that annual session. If the General Assembly is not in annual session or if the Executive Order is delivered after April 1, the General Assembly shall consider the Executive Order at its next annual session, in which case the Executive Order shall be deemed to have been delivered on the first day of that annual session. Such an Executive Order shall not become effective if, within 60 calendar days after its delivery to the General Assembly, either house disapproves the Executive Order by the record vote of a majority of the members elected. An Executive Order not so disapproved shall become effective by its terms but not less than 60 calendar days after its delivery to the General Assembly.

Section 12. Governor - Pardons

The Governor may grant reprieves, commutations and pardons, after conviction, for all offenses on such terms as he thinks proper. The manner of applying therefore may be regulated by law.

Section 13. Governor - Legislative Messages

The Governor, at the beginning of each annual session of the General Assembly and at the close of his term of office, shall report to the General Assembly on the condition of the State and recommend such measures as he deems desirable.

Section 14. Lieutenant Governor - Duties

The Lieutenant Governor shall perform the duties and exercise the powers in the Executive Branch that may be delegated to him by the Governor and that may be prescribed by law.

Section 15. Attorney General - Duties

The Attorney General shall be the legal officer of the State, and shall have the duties and powers that may be prescribed by law.

Section 16. Secretary of State - Duties

The Secretary of State shall maintain the official records of the acts of the General Assembly and such official records of the Executive Branch as provided by law. Such official records shall be available for inspection by the public. He shall keep the Great Seal of the State of Illinois and perform other duties that may be prescribed by law.

Section 17. Comptroller - Duties

The Comptroller, in accordance with law, shall maintain the State's central fiscal accounts, and order payments into and out of the funds held by the Treasurer.

Section 18. Treasurer - Duties

The Treasurer, in accordance with law, shall be responsible for the safekeeping and investment of monies and securities deposited with him, and for their disbursement upon order of the Comptroller.

Section 19. Records - Reports

All officers of the Executive Branch shall keep accounts and shall make such reports as may be required by law. They shall provide the Governor with information relating to their respective offices, either in writing under oath, or otherwise, as the Governor may require.

Section 20. Bond

Civil officers of the Executive Branch may be required by law to give reasonable bond or other security for the faithful performance of their duties. If any officer is in default of such a requirement, his office shall be deemed vacant.

Section 21. Compensation

Officers of the Executive Branch shall be paid salaries established by law and shall receive no other compensation for their services. Changes in the salaries of these officers elected or appointed for stated terms shall not take effect during the stated terms.

ARTICLE VI: THE JUDICIARY

Section 1. Courts

The judicial power is vested in a Supreme Court, an Appellate Court and Circuit Courts.

Section 2. Judicial Districts

The State is divided into five Judicial Districts for the selection of Supreme and Appellate Court Judges. The First Judicial District consists of Cook County. The remainder of the State shall be divided by law into four Judicial Districts of substantially equal population, each of which shall be compact and composed of contiguous counties.

Section 3. Supreme Court - Organization

The Supreme Court shall consist of seven Judges. Three shall be selected from the First Judicial District and one from each of the other Judicial Districts. Four Judges constitute a quorum and the concurrence of four is necessary for a decision. Supreme Court Judges shall select a Chief Justice from their number to serve for a term of three years.

Section 4. Supreme Court - Jurisdiction

(a) The Supreme Court may exercise original jurisdiction in cases relating to revenue, mandamus, prohibition or habeas corpus and as may be necessary to the complete determination of any case on review.

(b) Appeals from judgments of Circuit Courts imposing a sentence of death shall be directly to the Supreme Court as a matter of right. The Supreme Court shall provide by rule for direct appeal in other cases.

(c) Appeals from the Appellate Court to the Supreme Court are a matter of right if a question under the Constitution of the United States or of this State arises for the first time in and as a result of the action of the Appellate Court, or if a division of the Appellate Court certifies that a case decided by it involves a question of such importance that the case should be decided by the Supreme Court. The Supreme Court may provide by rule for appeals from the Appellate Court in other cases.

Section 5. Appellate Court - Organization

The number of Appellate Judges to be selected from each Judicial District shall be provided by law. The Supreme Court shall prescribe by rule the number of Appellate divisions in each Judicial District. Each Appellate division shall have at least three Judges. Assignments to divisions shall be made by the Supreme Court. A majority of a division constitutes a quorum and the concurrence of a majority of the division is necessary for a decision. There shall be at least one division in each Judicial District and each division shall sit at times and places prescribed by rules of the Supreme Court.

Section 6. Appellate Court - Jurisdiction

Appeals from final judgments of a Circuit Court are a matter of right to the Appellate Court in the Judicial District in which the Circuit Court is located except in cases appealable directly to the Supreme Court and except that after a trial on the merits in a criminal case, there shall be no appeal from a judgment of acquittal. The Supreme Court may provide by rule for appeals to the Appellate Court from other than final judgments of Circuit Courts. The Appellate Court may exercise original jurisdiction when necessary to the complete determination of any case on review. The Appellate Court shall have such powers of direct review of administrative action as provided by law.

Section 7. Judicial Circuits

(a) The State shall be divided into Judicial Circuits consisting of one or more counties. The First Judicial District shall constitute a Judicial Circuit. The Judicial Circuits within the other Judicial Districts shall be as provided by law. Circuits composed of more than one county shall be compact and of contiguous counties. The General Assembly by law may provide for the division of a circuit for the purpose of selection of Circuit Judges and for the selection of Circuit Judges from the circuit at large.

(b) Each Judicial Circuit shall have one Circuit Court with such number of Circuit Judges as provided by law. Unless otherwise provided by law, there shall be at least one Circuit Judge from each county. In the First Judicial District, unless otherwise provided by law, Cook County, Chicago, and the area outside Chicago shall be separate units for the selection of Circuit Judges, with at least twelve chosen at large from the area outside Chicago and at least thirty-six chosen at large from Chicago.

(c) Circuit Judges in each circuit shall select by secret ballot a Chief Judge from their number to serve at their pleasure. Subject to the authority of the Supreme Court, the Chief Judge shall have general administrative authority over his court, including authority to provide for divisions, general or specialized, and for appropriate times and places of holding court.

Section 8. Associate Judges

Each Circuit Court shall have such number of Associate Judges as provided by law. Associate Judges shall be appointed by the Circuit Judges in each circuit as the Supreme Court shall provide by rule. In the First Judicial District, unless otherwise provided by law, at least one-fourth of the Associate Judges shall be appointed from,

and reside, outside Chicago. The Supreme Court shall provide
by rule for matters to be assigned to Associate Judges.

Section 9. Circuit Courts - Jurisdiction

Circuit Courts shall have original jurisdiction of all
justiciable matters except when the Supreme Court has
original and exclusive jurisdiction relating to redistricting
of the General Assembly and to the ability of the Governor to
serve or resume office. Circuit Courts shall have such power
to review administrative action as provided by law.

Section 10. Terms Of Office

The terms of office of Supreme and Appellate Court Judges
shall be ten years; of Circuit Judges, six years; and of
Associate Judges, four years.

Section 11. Eligibility for Office

No person shall be eligible to be a Judge or Associate
Judge unless he is a United States citizen, a licensed
attorney-at-law of this State, and a resident of the unit
which selects him. No change in the boundaries of a unit
shall affect the tenure in office of a Judge or Associate
Judge incumbent at the time of such change.

Section 12. Election And Retention

(a) Supreme, Appellate and Circuit Judges shall be
nominated at primary elections or by petition. Judges shall
be elected at general or judicial elections as the General
Assembly shall provide by law. A person eligible for the
office of Judge may cause his name to appear on the ballot as
a candidate for Judge at the primary and at the general or
judicial elections by submitting petitions. The General
Assembly shall prescribe by law the requirements for
petitions.

(b) The office of a Judge shall be vacant upon his death, resignation, retirement, removal, or upon the conclusion of his term without retention in office. Whenever an additional Appellate or Circuit Judge is authorized by law, the office shall be filled in the manner provided for filling a vacancy in that office.

(c) A vacancy occurring in the office of Supreme, Appellate or Circuit Judge shall be filled as the General Assembly may provide by law. In the absence of a law, vacancies may be filled by appointment by the Supreme Court. A person appointed to fill a vacancy 60 or more days prior to the next primary election to nominate Judges shall serve until the vacancy is filled for a term at the next general or judicial election. A person appointed to fill a vacancy less than 60 days prior to the next primary election to nominate Judges shall serve until the vacancy is filled at the second general or judicial election following such appointment.

(d) Not less than six months before the general election preceding the expiration of his term of office, a Supreme, Appellate or Circuit Judge who has been elected to that office may file in the office of the Secretary of State a declaration of candidacy to succeed himself. The Secretary of State, not less than 63 days before the election, shall certify the Judge's candidacy to the proper election officials. The names of Judges seeking retention shall be submitted to the electors, separately and without party designation, on the sole question whether each Judge shall be retained in office for another term. The retention elections shall be conducted at general elections in the appropriate Judicial District, for Supreme and Appellate Judges, and in the circuit for Circuit Judges. The affirmative vote of three-fifths of the electors voting on the question shall elect the Judge to the office for a term commencing on the first Monday in December following his election.

(e) A law reducing the number of Appellate or Circuit Judges shall be without prejudice to the right of the Judges affected to seek retention in office. A reduction shall become effective when a vacancy occurs in the affected unit.

Section 13. Prohibited Activities

(a) The Supreme Court shall adopt rules of conduct for Judges and Associate Judges.

(b) Judges and Associate Judges shall devote full time to judicial duties. They shall not practice law, hold a position of profit, hold office under the United States or this State or unit of local government or school district or in a political party. Service in the State militia or armed forces of the United States for periods of time permitted by rule of the Supreme Court shall not disqualify a person from serving as a Judge or Associate Judge.

Section 14. Judicial Salaries And Expenses - Fee Officers Eliminated

Judges shall receive salaries provided by law which shall not be diminished to take effect during their terms of office. All salaries and such expenses as may be provided by law shall be paid by the State, except that Appellate, Circuit and Associate Judges shall receive such additional compensation from counties within their district or circuit as may be provided by law. There shall be no fee officers in the judicial system.

Section 15. Retirement - Discipline

(a) The General Assembly may provide by law for the retirement of Judges and Associate Judges at a prescribed age. Any retired Judge or Associate Judge, with his or her consent, may be assigned by the Supreme Court to judicial service for which he or she shall receive the applicable compensation in lieu of retirement benefits. A retired Associate Judge may be assigned only as an Associate Judge.

(b) A Judicial Inquiry Board is created. The Supreme Court shall select two Circuit Judges as members and the Governor shall appoint four persons who are not lawyers and three lawyers as members of the Board. No more than two of the lawyers and two of the non-lawyers appointed by the Governor shall be members of the same political party. The terms of Board members shall be four years. A vacancy on the Board shall be filled for a full term in the manner the original appointment was made. No member may serve on the Board more than eight years.

(c) The Board shall be convened permanently, with authority to conduct investigations, receive or initiate complaints concerning a Judge or Associate Judge, and file complaints with the Courts Commission. The Board shall not file a complaint unless five members believe that a reasonable basis exists:

(1) to charge the Judge or Associate Judge with willful misconduct in office, persistent failure to perform his duties, or other conduct that is prejudicial to the administration of justice or that brings the judicial office into disrepute, or

(2) to charge that the Judge or Associate Judge is physically or mentally unable to perform his duties. All proceedings of the Board shall be confidential except the filing of a complaint with the Courts Commission. The Board shall prosecute the complaint.

(d) The Board shall adopt rules governing its procedures. It shall have subpoena power and authority to appoint and direct its staff. Members of the Board who are not Judges shall receive per diem compensation and necessary expenses; members who are Judges shall receive necessary expenses only. The General Assembly by law shall appropriate funds for the operation of the Board.

(e) An independent Courts Commission is created consisting of one Supreme Court Judge selected by that Court as a member and one as an alternate, two Appellate Court Judges selected by that Court as members and three as alternates, two Circuit Judges selected by the Supreme Court as members and three as alternates, and two citizens selected by the Governor as members and two as alternates. Members and alternates who are Appellate Court Judges must each be from a different Judicial District. Members and alternates who are Circuit Judges must each be from a different Judicial District. Members and alternates of the Commission shall not be members of the Judicial Inquiry Board. The members of the Commission shall select a chairperson to serve a two-year term.

The Commission shall be convened permanently to hear complaints filed by the Judicial Inquiry Board. The Commission shall have authority after notice and public hearing:

(1) to remove from office, suspend without pay, censure or reprimand a Judge or Associate Judge for willful misconduct in office, persistent failure to perform his or her duties, or other conduct that is prejudicial to the administration of justice or that brings the judicial office into disrepute, or

(2) to suspend, with or without pay, or retire a Judge or Associate Judge who is physically or mentally unable to perform his or her duties.

(f) The concurrence of four members of the Commission shall be necessary for a decision. The decision of the Commission shall be final.

(g) The Commission shall adopt comprehensive rules to ensure that its procedures are fair and appropriate. These rules and any amendments shall be public and filed with the Secretary of State at least 30 days before becoming effective.

(h) A member of the Commission shall disqualify himself or herself, or the other members of the Commission shall disqualify a member, with respect to any proceeding in which disqualification or recusal would be required of a Judge under rules of the Supreme Court, under rules of the Commission, or by law.

If a Supreme Court Judge is the subject of a proceeding, then there shall be no Supreme Court Judge sitting as a member of the Commission with respect to that proceeding. Instead, an alternate Appellate Court Judge not from the same Judicial District as the subject Supreme Court Judge shall replace the subject Supreme Court Judge. If a member who is an Appellate Court Judge is the subject of a proceeding, then an alternate Appellate Court Judge shall replace the subject Appellate Court Judge. If an Appellate Court Judge who is not a member is the subject of a proceeding and an Appellate Court Judge from the same Judicial District is a member, then an alternate Appellate Court Judge shall replace that member. If a member who is a Circuit Judge is the subject of a proceeding, then an alternate Circuit Judge shall replace the subject Circuit Judge. If a Circuit Judge who is not a member is the subject of a proceeding and a Circuit Judge from the same Judicial District is a member, then an alternate Circuit Judge shall replace that member.

If a member of the Commission is disqualified under this Section with respect to any proceeding, that member shall be replaced by an alternate on a rotating basis in a manner provided by rule of the Commission. The alternate shall act as member of the Commission with respect to that proceeding only.

(i) The Commission shall have power to issue subpoenas.

(j) Members and alternates of the Commission who are not Judges shall receive per diem compensation and necessary expenses; members and alternates who are Judges shall receive necessary expenses only. The General Assembly shall provide by law for the expenses and compensation of the Commission.

Section 16. Administration

General administrative and supervisory authority over all courts is vested in the Supreme Court and shall be exercised by the Chief Justice in accordance with its rules. The Supreme Court shall appoint an administrative director and staff, who shall serve at its pleasure, to assist the Chief Justice in his duties. The Supreme Court may assign a Judge temporarily to any court and an Associate Judge to serve temporarily as an Associate Judge on any Circuit Court. The Supreme Court shall provide by rule for expeditious and inexpensive appeals.

Section 17. Judicial Conference

The Supreme Court shall provide by rule for an annual judicial conference to consider the work of the courts and to suggest improvements in the administration of justice and shall report thereon annually in writing to the General Assembly not later than January 31.

Section 18. Clerks Of Courts

(a) The Supreme Court and the Appellate Court Judges of each Judicial District, respectively, shall appoint a clerk and other non-judicial officers for their Court or District.

(b) The General Assembly shall provide by law for the election, or for the appointment by Circuit Judges, of clerks and other non-judicial officers of the Circuit Courts and for their terms of office and removal for cause.

(c) The salaries of clerks and other non-judicial officers shall be as provided by law.

Section 19. State's Attorneys - Selection, Salary

A State's Attorney shall be elected in each county in 1972 and every fourth year thereafter for a four year term. One State's Attorney may be elected to serve two or more counties if the governing boards of such counties so provide and a majority of the electors of each county voting on the issue approve. A person shall not be eligible for the office of State's Attorney unless he is a United States citizen and a licensed attorney-at-law of this State. His salary shall be provided by law.

ARTICLE VII: LOCAL GOVERNMENT

Section 1. Municipalities and Units of Local Government

"Municipalities" means cities, villages and incorporated towns. "Units of local government" means counties, municipalities, townships, special districts, and units, designated as units of local government by law, which exercise limited governmental powers or powers in respect to limited governmental subjects, but does not include school districts.

Section 2. County Territory, Boundaries and Seats

(a) The General Assembly shall provide by law for the formation, consolidation, merger, division, and dissolution of counties, and for the transfer of territory between counties.

(b) County boundaries shall not be changed unless approved by referendum in each county affected.

(c) County seats shall not be changed unless approved by three-fifths of those voting on the question in a county-wide referendum.

Section 3. County Boards

(a) A county board shall be elected in each county. The number of members of the county board shall be fixed by ordinance in each county within limitations provided by law.

(b) The General Assembly by law shall provide methods available to all counties for the election of county board members. No county, other than Cook County, may change its method of electing board members except as approved by county-wide referendum.

(c) Members of the Cook County Board shall be elected from two districts, Chicago and that part of Cook County outside Chicago, unless:

(1) a different method of election is approved by a majority of votes cast in each of the two districts in a county-wide referendum or

(2) the Cook County Board by ordinance divides the county into single member districts from which members of the County Board resident in each district are elected. If a different method of election is adopted pursuant to option (1) the method of election may thereafter be altered only pursuant to option (2) or by county-wide referendum. A different method of election may be adopted pursuant to option (2) only once and the method of election may thereafter be altered only by county-wide referendum.

Section 4. County Officers

(a) Any county may elect a chief executive officer as provided by law. He shall have those duties and powers provided by law and those provided by county ordinance.

(b) The President of the Cook County Board shall be elected from the County at large and shall be the chief executive officer of the County. If authorized by county ordinance, a person seeking election as President of the Cook County Board may also seek election as a member of the Board.

(c) Each county shall elect a sheriff, county clerk and treasurer and may elect or appoint a coroner, recorder, assessor, auditor and such other officers as provided by law or by county ordinance. Except as changed pursuant to this Section, elected county officers shall be elected for terms of four years at general elections as provided by law. Any office may be created or eliminated and the terms of office and manner of selection changed by county-wide referendum.

Offices other than sheriff, county clerk and treasurer may be eliminated and the terms of office and manner of selection changed by law. Offices other than sheriff, county clerk, treasurer, coroner, recorder, assessor and auditor may be eliminated and the terms of office and manner of selection changed by county ordinance.

(d) County officers shall have those duties, powers and functions provided by law and those provided by county ordinance. County officers shall have the duties, powers or functions derived from common law or historical precedent unless altered by law or county ordinance.

(e) The county treasurer or the person designated to perform his functions may act as treasurer of any unit of local government and any school district in his county when requested by any such unit or school district and shall so act when required to do so by law.

Section 5. Townships

The General Assembly shall provide by law for the formation of townships in any county when approved by county-wide referendum. Townships may be consolidated or merged, and one or more townships may be dissolved or divided, when approved by referendum in each township affected. All townships in a county may be dissolved when approved by a referendum in the total area in which township officers are elected.

Section 6. Powers Of Home Rule Units

(a) A County which has a chief executive officer elected by the electors of the county and any municipality which has a population of more than 25,000 are home rule units. Other municipalities may elect by referendum to become home rule units. Except as limited by this Section, a home rule unit may exercise any power and perform any function pertaining to its government and affairs including, but not limited to, the power to regulate for the protection of the public health, safety, morals and welfare; to license; to tax; and to incur debt.

(b) A home rule unit by referendum may elect not to be a home rule unit.

(c) If a home rule county ordinance conflicts with an ordinance of a municipality, the municipal ordinance shall prevail within its jurisdiction.

(d) A home rule unit does not have the power:

(1) to incur debt payable from ad valorem property tax receipts maturing more than 40 years from the time it is incurred or

(2) to define and provide for the punishment of a felony.

(e) A home rule unit shall have only the power that the General Assembly may provide by law:

(1) to punish by imprisonment for more than six months or

(2) to license for revenue or impose taxes upon or measured by income or earnings or upon occupations.

(f) A home rule unit shall have the power subject to approval by referendum to adopt, alter or repeal a form of government provided by law, except that the form of government of Cook County shall be subject to the provisions of Section 3 of this Article. A home rule municipality shall have the power to provide for its officers, their manner of selection and terms of office only as approved by referendum or as otherwise authorized by law. A home rule county shall have the power to provide for its officers, their manner of selection and terms of office in the manner set forth in Section 4 of this Article.

(g) The General Assembly by a law approved by the vote of three-fifths of the members elected to each house may deny or limit the power to tax and any other power or function of a home rule unit not exercised or performed by the State other than a power or function specified in subsection (l) of this section.

(h) The General Assembly may provide specifically by law for the exclusive exercise by the State of any power or function of a home rule unit other than a taxing power or a power or function specified in subsection (l) of this Section.

(i) Home rule units may exercise and perform concurrently with the State any power or function of a home rule unit to the extent that the General Assembly by law does not specifically limit the concurrent exercise or specifically declare the State's exercise to be exclusive.

(j) The General Assembly may limit by law the amount of debt which home rule counties may incur and may limit by law approved by three-fifths of the members elected to each house the amount of debt, other than debt payable from ad valorem property tax receipts, which home rule municipalities may incur.

(k) The General Assembly may limit by law the amount and require referendum approval of debt to be incurred by home rule municipalities, payable from ad valorem property tax receipts, only in excess of the following percentages of the assessed value of its taxable property: (1) if its population is 500,000 or more, an aggregate of three percent; (2) if its population is more than 25,000 and less than 500,000, an aggregate of one percent; and (3) if its population is 25,000 or less, an aggregate of one-half percent. Indebtedness which is outstanding on the effective date of this Constitution or which is thereafter approved by referendum or assumed from another unit of local government shall not be included in the foregoing percentage amounts.

(l) The General Assembly may not deny or limit the power of home rule units (1) to make local improvements by special assessment and to exercise this power jointly with other counties and municipalities, and other classes of units of local government having that power on the effective date of this Constitution unless that power is subsequently denied by law to any such other units of local government or (2) to levy or impose additional taxes upon areas within their boundaries in the manner provided by law for the provision of special services to those areas and for the payment of debt incurred in order to provide those special services.

(m) Powers and functions of home rule units shall be construed liberally.

Section 7. Counties and Municipalities Other Than Home Rule Units

Counties and municipalities which are not home rule units shall have only powers granted to them by law and the powers:

(1) to make local improvements by special assessment and to exercise this power jointly with other counties and municipalities, and other classes of units of local government having that power on the effective date of this Constitution unless that power is subsequently denied by law to any such other units of local government;

(2) by referendum, to adopt, alter or repeal their forms of government provided by law;

(3) in the case of municipalities, to provide by referendum for their officers, manner of selection and terms of office;

(4) in the case of counties, to provide for their officers, manner of selection and terms of office as provided in Section 4 of this Article;

(5) to incur debt except as limited by law and except that debt payable from ad valorem property tax receipts shall mature within 40 years from the time it is incurred; and (6) to levy or impose additional taxes upon areas within their boundaries in the manner provided by law for the provision of special services to those areas and for the payment of debt incurred in order to provide those special services.

Section 8. Powers and Officers of School Districts and Units of Local Government Other Than Counties and Municipalities

Townships, school districts, special districts and units, designated by law as units of local government, which exercise limited governmental powers or powers in respect to limited governmental subjects shall have only powers granted by law. No law shall grant the power:

(1) to any of the foregoing units to incur debt payable from ad valorem property tax receipts maturing more than 40 years from the time it is incurred, or

(2) to make improvements by special assessments to any of the foregoing classes of units which do not have that power on the effective date of this Constitution. The General Assembly shall provide by law for the selection of officers of the foregoing units, but the officers shall not be appointed by any person in the Judicial Branch.

Section 9. Salaries and Fees

(a) Compensation of officers and employees and the office expenses of units of local government shall not be paid from fees collected. Fees may be collected as provided by law and by ordinance and shall be deposited upon receipt with the treasurer of the unit. Fees shall not be based upon funds disbursed or collected, nor upon the levy or extension of taxes.

(b) An increase or decrease in the salary of an elected officer of any unit of local government shall not take effect during the term for which that officer is elected.

Section 10. Intergovernmental Cooperation

(a) Units of local government and school districts may contract or otherwise associate among themselves, with the State, with other states and their units of local government and school districts, and with the United States to obtain or share services and to exercise, combine, or transfer any power or function, in any manner not prohibited by law or by ordinance. Units of local government and school districts may contract and otherwise associate with individuals, associations, and corporations in any manner not prohibited by law or by ordinance. Participating units of government may use their credit, revenues, and other resources to pay costs and to service debt related to intergovernmental activities.

(b) Officers and employees of units of local government and school districts may participate in intergovernmental activities authorized by their units of government without relinquishing their offices or positions.

(c) The State shall encourage intergovernmental cooperation and use its technical and financial resources to assist intergovernmental activities.

Section 11. Initiative and Referendum

(a) Proposals for actions which are authorized by this Article or by law and which require approval by referendum may be initiated and submitted to the electors by resolution of the governing board of a unit of local government or by petition of electors in the manner provided by law.

(b) Referenda required by this Article shall be held at general elections, except as otherwise provided by law. Questions submitted to referendum shall be adopted if approved by a majority of those voting on the question unless a different requirement is specified in this Article.

Section 12. Implementation of Governmental Changes

The General Assembly shall provide by law for the transfer of assets, powers and functions, and for the payment of outstanding debt in connection with the formation, consolidation, merger, division, dissolution and change in the boundaries of units of local government.

ARTICLE VIII: FINANCE

Section 1. General Provisions

(a) Public funds, property or credit shall be used only for public purposes.

(b) The State, units of local government and school districts shall incur obligations for payment or make payments from public funds only as authorized by law or ordinance.

(c) Reports and records of the obligation, receipt and use of public funds of the State, units of local government and school districts are public records available for inspection by the public according to law.

Section 2. State Finance

(a) The Governor shall prepare and submit to the General Assembly, at a time prescribed by law, a State budget for the ensuing fiscal year. The budget shall set forth the estimated balance of funds available for appropriation at the beginning of the fiscal year, the estimated receipts, and a plan for expenditures and obligations during the fiscal year of every department, authority, public corporation and quasi-public corporation of the State, every State college and university, and every other public agency created by the State, but not of units of local government or school districts. The budget shall also set forth the indebtedness and contingent liabilities of the State and such other information as may be required by law. Proposed expenditures shall not exceed funds estimated to be available for the fiscal year as shown in the budget.

(b) The General Assembly by law shall make appropriations for all expenditures of public funds by the State. Appropriations for a fiscal year shall not exceed funds estimated by the General Assembly to be available during that year.

Section 3. State Audit and Auditor General

(a) The General Assembly shall provide by law for the audit of the obligation, receipt and use of public funds of the State. The General Assembly, by a vote of three-fifths of the members elected to each house, shall appoint an Auditor General and may remove him for cause by a similar vote. The Auditor General shall serve for a term of ten years. His compensation shall be established by law and shall not be diminished, but may be increased, to take effect during his term.

(b) The Auditor General shall conduct the audit of public funds of the State. He shall make additional reports and investigations as directed by the General Assembly. He shall report his findings and recommendations to the General Assembly and to the Governor.

Section 4. Systems of Accounting, Auditing and Reporting

The General Assembly by law shall provide systems of accounting, auditing and reporting of the obligation, receipt and use of public funds. These systems shall be used by all units of local government and school districts.

ARTICLE IX: REVENUE

Section 1. State Revenue Power

The General Assembly has the exclusive power to raise revenue by law except as limited or otherwise provided in this Constitution. The power of taxation shall not be surrendered, suspended, or contracted away.

Section 2. Non-Property Taxes – Classification, Exemptions, Deductions, Allowances and Credits

In any law classifying the subjects or objects of non-property taxes or fees, the classes shall be reasonable and the subjects and objects within each class shall be taxed uniformly. Exemptions, deductions, credits, refunds and other allowances shall be reasonable.

Section 3. Limitations on Income Taxation

(a) A tax on or measured by income shall be at a non-graduated rate. At any one time there may be no more than one such tax imposed by the State for State purposes on individuals and one such tax so imposed on corporations. In any such tax imposed upon corporations the rate shall not exceed the rate imposed on individuals by more than a ratio of 8 to 5.

(b) Laws imposing taxes on or measured by income may adopt by reference provisions of the laws and regulations of the United States, as they then exist or thereafter may be changed, for the purpose of arriving at the amount of income upon which the tax is imposed.

Section 4. Real Property Taxation

(a) Except as otherwise provided in this Section, taxes upon real property shall be levied uniformly by valuation ascertained as the General Assembly shall provide by law.

(b) Subject to such limitations as the General Assembly may hereafter prescribe by law, counties with a population of more than 200,000 may classify or continue to classify real property for purposes of taxation. Any such classification shall be reasonable and assessments shall be uniform within each class. The level of assessment or rate of tax of the highest class in a county shall not exceed two and one-half times the level of assessment or rate of tax of the lowest class in that county. Real property used in farming in a county shall not be assessed at a higher level of assessment than single family residential real property in that county.

(c) Any depreciation in the value of real estate occasioned by a public easement may be deducted in assessing such property.

Section 5. Personal Property Taxation

(a) The General Assembly by law may classify personal property for purposes of taxation by valuation, abolish such taxes on any or all classes and authorize the levy of taxes in lieu of the taxation of personal property by valuation.

(b) Any ad valorem personal property tax abolished on or before the effective date of this Constitution shall not be reinstated.

(c) On or before January 1, 1979, the General Assembly by law shall abolish all ad valorem personal property taxes and concurrently therewith and thereafter shall replace all revenue lost by units of local government and school districts as a result of the abolition of ad valorem personal property taxes subsequent to January 2, 1971. Such revenue shall be replaced by imposing statewide taxes, other than ad valorem taxes on real estate, solely on those classes relieved of the burden of paying ad valorem personal property taxes because of the abolition of such taxes subsequent to January 2, 1971. If any taxes imposed for such replacement purposes are taxes on or measured by income, such replacement taxes shall not be considered for purposes of the limitations of one tax and the ratio of 8 to 5 set forth in Section 3(a) of this Article.

Section 6. Exemptions From Property Taxation

The General Assembly by law may exempt from taxation only the property of the State, units of local government and school districts and property used exclusively for agricultural and horticultural societies, and for school, religious, cemetery and charitable purposes. The General Assembly by law may grant homestead exemptions or rent credits.

Section 7. Overlapping Taxing Districts

The General Assembly may provide by law for fair apportionment of the burden of taxation of property situated in taxing districts that lie in more than one county.

Section 8. Tax Sales

(a) Real property shall not be sold for the nonpayment of taxes or special assessments without judicial proceedings.

(b) The right of redemption from all sales of real estate for the nonpayment of taxes or special assessments, except as provided in subsections (c) and (d), shall exist in favor of owners and persons interested in such real estate for not less than 2 years following such sales.

(c) The right of redemption from the sale for nonpayment of taxes or special assessments of a parcel of real estate which:

(1) is vacant non-farm real estate or

(2) contains an improvement consisting of a structure or structures each of which contains 7 or more residential units or

(3) is commercial or industrial property; shall exist in favor of owners and persons interested in such real estate for not less than one year following such sales.

(d) The right of redemption from the sale for nonpayment of taxes or special assessments of a parcel real estate which:

(1) is vacant non-farm real estate or

(2) contains an improvement consisting of a structure or structures each of which contains 7 or more residential units or

(3) is commercial or industrial property; and upon which all or a part of the general taxes for each of 2 or more years are delinquent shall exist in favor of owners and persons interested in such real estate for not less than 6 months following such sales.

(e) Owners, occupants and parties interested shall be given reasonable notice of the sale and the date of expiration of the period of redemption as the General Assembly provides by law.

Section 9. State Debt

(a) No State debt shall be incurred except as provided in this Section. For the purpose of this Section, "State debt" means bonds or other evidences of indebtedness which are secured by the full faith and credit of the State or are required to be repaid, directly or indirectly, from tax revenue and which are incurred by the State, any department, authority, public corporation or quasi-public corporation of the State, any State college or university, or any other public agency created by the State, but not by units of local government, or school districts.

(b) State debt for specific purposes may be incurred or the payment of State or other debt guaranteed in such amounts as may be provided either in a law passed by the vote of three-fifths of the members elected to each house of the General Assembly or in a law approved by a majority of the electors voting on the question at the next general election following passage. Any law providing for the incurring or guaranteeing of debt shall set forth the specific purposes and the manner of repayment.

(c) State debt in anticipation of revenues to be collected in a fiscal year may be incurred by law in an amount not exceeding 5% of the State's appropriations for that fiscal year. Such debt shall be retired from the revenues realized in that fiscal year.

(d) State debt may be incurred by law in an amount not exceeding 15% of the State's appropriations for that fiscal year to meet deficits caused by emergencies or failures of revenue. Such law shall provide that the debt be repaid within one year of the date it is incurred.

(e) State debt may be incurred by law to refund outstanding State debt if the refunding debt matures within the term of the outstanding State debt.

(f) The State, departments, authorities, public corporations and quasi-public corporations of the State, the State colleges and universities and other public agencies created by the State, may issue bonds or other evidences of indebtedness which are not secured by the full faith and credit or tax revenue of the State nor required to be repaid, directly or indirectly, from tax revenue, for such purposes and in such amounts as may be authorized by law.

Section 10. Revenue Article Not Limited

This Article is not qualified or limited by the provisions of Article VII of this Constitution concerning the size of the majorities in the General Assembly necessary to deny or limit the power to tax granted to units of local government.

Section 11. Transportation Funds

(a) No moneys, including bond proceeds, derived from taxes, fees, excises, or license taxes relating to registration, title, or operation or use of vehicles, or related to the use of highways, roads, streets, bridges, mass transit, intercity passenger rail, ports, airports, or to fuels used for propelling vehicles, or derived from taxes, fees, excises, or license taxes relating to any other transportation infrastructure or transportation operation, shall be expended for purposes other than as provided in subsections (b) and (c).

(b) Transportation funds may be expended for the following: the costs of administering laws related to vehicles and transportation, including statutory refunds and adjustments provided in those laws; payment of highway obligations; costs for construction, reconstruction, maintenance, repair, and betterment of highways, roads, streets, bridges, mass transit, intercity passenger rail, ports, airports, or other forms of transportation; and other statutory highway purposes. Transportation funds may also be expended for the State or local share of highway funds to match federal aid highway funds, and expenses of grade separation of highways and railroad crossings, including protection of at-grade highways and railroad crossings, and, with respect to local governments, other transportation purposes as authorized by law.

(c) The costs of administering laws related to vehicles and transportation shall be limited to direct program expenses related to the following: the enforcement of traffic, railroad, and motor carrier laws; the safety of highways, roads, streets, bridges, mass transit, intercity passenger rail, ports, or airports; and the construction, reconstruction, improvement, repair, maintenance, operation, and administration of highways, under any related provisions of law or any purpose related or incident to, including grade separation of highways and railroad crossings. The limitations to the costs of administering laws related to vehicles and transportation under this subsection (c) shall also include direct program expenses related to workers' compensation claims for death or injury of employees of the State's transportation agency; the acquisition of land and the erection of buildings for highway purposes, including the acquisition of highway rights-of-way or for investigations to determine the reasonable anticipated future highway needs; and the making of surveys, plans, specifications, and estimates for the construction and maintenance of flight strips and highways. The expenses related to the construction and maintenance of flight strips and highways under this subsection (c) are for the purpose of providing access to military and naval reservations, defense-industries, defense-industry sites, and sources of raw materials, including the replacement of existing highways and highway connections shut off from general use at military and naval reservations, defense-industries, and defense-industry sites, or the purchase of rights-of-way.

(d) None of the revenues described in subsection (a) of this Section shall, by transfer, offset, or otherwise, be diverted to any purpose other than those described in subsections (b) and (c) of this Section.

(e) If the General Assembly appropriates funds for a mode of transportation not described in this Section, the General Assembly must provide for a dedicated source of funding.

(f) Federal funds may be spent for any purposes authorized by federal law.

ARTICLE X: EDUCATION

Section 1. Goal - Free Schools

A fundamental goal of the People of the State is the educational development of all persons to the limits of their capacities.

The State shall provide for an efficient system of high quality public educational institutions and services. Education in public schools through the secondary level shall be free. There may be such other free education as the General Assembly provides by law.

The State has the primary responsibility for financing the system of public education.

Section 2. State Board of Education - Chief State Educational Officer

(a) There is created a State Board of Education to be elected or selected on a regional basis. The number of members, their qualifications, terms of office and manner of election or selection shall be provided by law. The Board, except as limited by law, may establish goals, determine policies, provide for planning and evaluating education programs and recommend financing. The Board shall have such other duties and powers as provided by law.

(b) The State Board of Education shall appoint a chief state educational officer.

Section 3. Public Funds for Sectarian Purposes Forbidden

Neither the General Assembly nor any county, city, town, township, school district, or other public corporation, shall ever make any appropriation or pay from any public fund whatever, anything in aid of any church or sectarian purpose, or to help support or sustain any school, academy, seminary, college, university, or other literary or scientific institution, controlled by any church or sectarian denomination whatever; nor shall any grant or donation of land, money, or other personal property ever be made by the State, or any such public corporation, to any church, or for any sectarian purpose.

ARTICLE XI: ENVIRONMENT

Section 1. Public Policy - Legislative Responsibility

The public policy of the State and the duty of each
person is to provide and maintain a healthful environment for
the benefit of this and future generations. The General
Assembly shall provide by law for the implementation and
enforcement of this public policy.

Section 2. Rights of Individuals

Each person has the right to a healthful environment.
Each person may enforce this right against any party,
governmental or private, through appropriate legal
proceedings subject to reasonable limitation and regulation
as the General Assembly may provide by law.

ARTICLE XII: MILITIA

Section 1. Membership

The State militia consists of all able-bodied persons residing in the State except those exempted by law.

Section 2. Subordination of Military Power

The military shall be in strict subordination to the civil power.

Section 3. Organization, Equipment and Discipline

The General Assembly shall provide by law for the organization, equipment and discipline of the militia in conformity with the laws governing the armed forces of the United States.

Section 4. Commander-In-Chief and Officers

(a) The Governor is commander-in-chief of the organized militia, except when they are in the service of the United States. He may call them out to enforce the laws, suppress insurrection or repel invasion.

(b) The Governor shall commission militia officers who shall hold their commissions for such time as may be provided by law.

Section 5. Privilege From Arrest

Except in cases of treason, felony or breach of peace, persons going to, returning from or on militia duty are privileged from arrest.

ARTICLE XIII: GENERAL PROVISIONS

Section 1. Disqualification for Public Office

A person convicted of a felony, bribery, perjury or other infamous crime shall be ineligible to hold an office created by this Constitution. Eligibility may be restored as provided by law.

Section 2. Statement of Economic Interests

All candidates for or holders of state offices and all members of a Commission or Board created by this Constitution shall file a verified statement of their economic interests, as provided by law. The General Assembly by law may impose a similar requirement upon candidates for, or holders of, offices in units of local government and school districts. Statements shall be filed annually with the Secretary of State and shall be available for inspection by the public. The General Assembly by law shall prescribe a reasonable time for filing the statement. Failure to file a statement within the time prescribed shall result in ineligibility for, or forfeiture of, office. This Section shall not be construed as limiting the authority of any branch of government to establish and enforce ethical standards for that branch.

Section 3. Oath or Affirmation of Office

Each prospective holder of a State office or other State position created by this Constitution, before taking office, shall take and subscribe to the following oath or affirmation:

   "I do solemnly swear (affirm) that I will support the Constitution of the United States, and the Constitution of the State of Illinois, and that I will faithfully discharge the duties of the office of .... to the best of my ability."

Section 4. Sovereign Immunity Abolished

Except as the General Assembly may provide by law, sovereign immunity in this State is abolished.

Section 5. Pension and Retirement Rights

Membership in any pension or retirement system of the State, any unit of local government or school district, or any agency or instrumentality thereof, shall be an enforceable contractual relationship, the benefits of which shall not be diminished or impaired.

Section 6. Corporations

Corporate charters shall be granted, amended, dissolved, or extended only pursuant to general laws.

Section 7. Public Transportation

Public transportation is an essential public purpose for which public funds may be expended. The General Assembly by law may provide for, aid, and assist public transportation, including the granting of public funds or credit to any corporation or public authority authorized to provide public transportation within the State.

Section 8. Branch Banking

Branch banking shall be authorized only by law approved by three-fifths of the members voting on the question or a majority of the members elected, whichever is greater, in each house of the General Assembly.

ARTICLE XIV: CONSTITUTIONAL REVISION

Section 1. Constitutional Convention

(a) Whenever three-fifths of the members elected to each house of the General Assembly so direct, the question of whether a Constitutional Convention should be called shall be submitted to the electors at the general election next occurring at least six months after such legislative direction.

(b) If the question of whether a Convention should be called is not submitted during any twenty-year period, the Secretary of State shall submit such question at the general election in the twentieth year following the last submission.

(c) The vote on whether to call a Convention shall be on a separate ballot. A Convention shall be called if approved by three-fifths of those voting on the question or a majority of those voting in the election.

(d) The General Assembly, at the session following approval by the electors, by law shall provide for the Convention and for the election of two delegates from each Legislative District; designate the time and place of the Convention's first meeting which shall be within three months after the election of delegates; fix and provide for the pay of delegates and officers; and provide for expenses necessarily incurred by the Convention.

(e) To be eligible to be a delegate a person must meet the same eligibility requirements as a member of the General Assembly. Vacancies shall be filled as provided by law.

(f) The Convention shall prepare such revision of or amendments to the Constitution as it deems necessary. Any proposed revision or amendments approved by a majority of the delegates elected shall be submitted to the electors in such manner as the Convention determines, at an election designated or called by the Convention occurring not less than two nor more than six months after the Convention's adjournment. Any revision or amendments proposed by the Convention shall be published with explanations, as the Convention provides, at least one month preceding the election.

(g) The vote on the proposed revision or amendments shall be on a separate ballot. Any proposed revision or amendments shall become effective, as the Convention provides, if approved by a majority of those voting on the question.

Section 2. Amendments by General Assembly

(a) Amendments to this Constitution may be initiated in either house of the General Assembly. Amendments shall be read in full on three different days in each house and reproduced before the vote is taken on final passage. Amendments approved by the vote of three-fifths of the members elected to each house shall be submitted to the electors at the general election next occurring at least six months after such legislative approval, unless withdrawn by a vote of a majority of the members elected to each house.

(b) Amendments proposed by the General Assembly shall be published with explanations, as provided by law, at least one month preceding the vote thereon by the electors. The vote on the proposed amendment or amendments shall be on a separate ballot. A proposed amendment shall become effective as the amendment provides if approved by either three-fifths of those voting on the question or a majority of those voting in the election.

(c) The General Assembly shall not submit proposed amendments to more than three Articles of the Constitution at any one election. No amendment shall be proposed or submitted under this Section from the time a Convention is called until after the electors have voted on the revision or amendments, if any, proposed by such Convention.

Section 3. Constitutional Initiative for Legislative Article

Amendments to Article IV of this Constitution may be proposed by a petition signed by a number of electors equal in number to at least eight percent of the total votes cast for candidates for Governor in the preceding gubernatorial election. Amendments shall be limited to structural and procedural subjects contained in Article IV. A petition shall contain the text of the proposed amendment and the date of the general election at which the proposed amendment is to be submitted, shall have been signed by the petitioning electors not more than twenty-four months preceding that general election and shall be filed with the Secretary of State at least six months before that general election. The procedure for determining the validity and sufficiency of a petition shall be provided by law. If the petition is valid and sufficient, the proposed amendment shall be submitted to the electors at that general election and shall become effective if approved by either three-fifths of those voting on the amendment or a majority of those voting in the election.

Section 4. Amendments to the Constitution of the United States

The affirmative vote of three-fifths of the members elected to each house of the General Assembly shall be required to request Congress to call a Federal Constitutional Convention, to ratify a proposed amendment to the Constitution of the United States, or to call a State Convention to ratify a proposed amendment to the Constitution of the United States. The General Assembly shall not take

action on any proposed amendment to the Constitution of the
United States submitted for ratification by legislatures
unless a majority of the members of the General Assembly
shall have been elected after the proposed amendment has been
submitted for ratification. The requirements of this Section
shall govern to the extent that they are not inconsistent
with requirements established by the United States.

SCHEDULE

The following Schedule Provisions shall remain part of this Constitution until their terms have been executed. Once each year the Attorney General shall review the following provisions and certify to the Secretary of State which, if any, have been executed. Any provisions so certified shall thereafter be removed from the Schedule and no longer published as part of this Constitution.

Section 1. (Removed)
Section 2. Prospective Operation of Bill of Rights.
Section 3. (Removed)
Section 4. Judicial Offices.
Section 5. Local Government.
Section 6. Authorized Bonds.
Section 7. (Removed)
Section 8. Cumulative Voting for Directors.
Section 9. General Transition.
Section 10. (Removed)

Section 2. Prospective Operation of Bill of Rights

Any rights, procedural or substantive, created for the first time by Article I shall be prospective and not retroactive.

Section 4. Judicial Offices

(a) On the effective date of this Constitution, Associate Judges and magistrates shall become Circuit Judges and Associate Judges, respectively, of their Circuit Courts. All laws and rules of court theretofore applicable to Associate Judges and magistrates shall remain in force and be applicable to the persons in their new offices until changed by the General Assembly or the Supreme Court, as the case may be.

(b) (Removed)

(c) (Removed)

(d) Until otherwise provided by law and except to the extent that the authority is inconsistent with Section 8 of Article VII, the Circuit Courts shall continue to exercise the non-judicial functions vested by law as of December 31, 1963, in county courts or the judges thereof.

Section 5. Local Government

(a) The number of members of a county board in a county which, as of the effective date of this Constitution, elects three members at large may be changed only as approved by county-wide referendum. If the number of members of such a county board is changed by county-wide referendum, the provisions of Section 3(a) of Article VII relating to the number of members of a county board shall govern thereafter.

(b) In Cook County, until (1) a method of election of county board members different from the method in existence on the effective date of this Constitution is approved by a majority of votes cast both in Chicago and in the area outside Chicago in a county-wide referendum or (2) the Cook County Board by ordinance divides the county into single member districts from which members of the County Board resident in each district are elected, the number of members of the Cook County Board shall be fifteen except that the county board may increase the number if necessary to comply with apportionment requirements. If either of the foregoing changes is made, the provisions of Section 3(a) of Article VII shall apply thereafter to Cook County.

(c) Townships in existence on the effective date of this Constitution are continued until consolidated, merged, divided or dissolved in accordance with Section 5 of Article VII.

Section 6. Authorized Bonds

Nothing in Section 9 of Article IX shall be construed to limit or impair the power to issue bonds or other evidences of indebtedness authorized but unissued on the effective date of this Constitution.

Section 8. Cumulative Voting for Directors

Shareholders of all corporations heretofore organized under any law of this State which requires cumulative voting of shares for corporate directors shall retain their right to vote cumulatively for such directors.

Section 9. General Transition

The rights and duties of all public bodies shall remain as if this Constitution had not been adopted with the exception of such changes as are contained in this Constitution. All laws, ordinances, regulations and rules of court not contrary to, or inconsistent with, the provisions of this Constitution shall remain in force, until they shall expire by their own limitation or shall be altered or repealed pursuant to this Constitution. The validity of all public and private bonds, debts and contracts, and of all suits, actions and rights of action, shall continue as if no change had taken place. All officers filling any office by election or appointment shall continue to exercise the duties thereof, until their offices shall have been abolished or their successors selected and qualified in accordance with this Constitution or laws enacted pursuant thereto.